FROM THE EDGE OF CHAOS AND FORM

FROM THE EDGE OF CHAOS AND FORM

Lynne Goldsmith

TRANSNATIONAL PRESS LONDON
2024

Poetry: 1

From the Edge of Chaos and Form

By Lynne Goldsmith

Copyright © 2024 Transnational Press London

All rights reserved. This book or any portion thereof may not be reproduced or used in any manner whatsoever without the express written permission of the publisher except for the use of brief quotations in a book review or scholarly journal.

First Published in 2024 by TRANSNATIONAL PRESS LONDON in the United Kingdom, 13 Stamford Place, Sale, M33 3BT, UK.
www.tplondon.com

Transnational Press London® and the logo and its affiliated brands are registered trademarks.

Requests for permission to reproduce material from this work should be sent to: sales@tplondon.com

Paperback
ISBN: 978-1-80135-259-8
Digital
ISBN: 978-1-80135-260-4

Cover Design: Nihal Yazgan
Cover image: The Forest Fire by Piero di Cosimo (1462-1522), Ashmolean Museum, Oxford.

www.tplondon.com

Contents

Preface 1
Signs of Creation 3
Universe of Patterns 15
Drifting 23
In Motion 41
Interspecies Interacting 67
Dear Killer 77
Myth and Artifact 97
Liminal Spaces 111
Acknowledgments 129

Preface

Edward Lorenz, meteorologist, professor and mathematician, discovered that seemingly insignificant motions/change can activate huge outcomes. His 'butterfly effect' (with the flap of a butterfly wing later causing a tornado in a distant location) illustrates the notion of chaos theory with future predictions being practically impossible and chaotic systems being non-linear, such as seen in the weather where no two weather days or snowflake designs are ever quite replicated. Emergence is a system created from the actions of individual parts that are supposedly lacking any central plan. Yet hidden within the chaos that is everywhere, surprising patterns are found.

Signs of Creation

Earth Native

Earth is where you stand
is where we're going under,
this ground made of
third planet from the sun
I am in wonder–

four and a half billion years old,
most species extinct in that time
of mostly water bodies
above liquid outer core

affecting magnetic field
I am drawn to pulled towards
no leaving atoms behind
all this energy will go on

in the death, the photons of
bounce
off to detectors of particle,
neurons

electromagnetically charged,
everything staying alive
how even Earth's core

iron made (slight alloy)
helps magnetic field
keep away sun's harm,
certain area melt–

other pressures
too great–
for heaviness
sinking
to cooling's

From the Edge of Chaos and Form

growing center

hard to believe
what goes on–
under all
the Earth's layers.

Points of Ignition

I. The Wildness of Fires

It starts as flame until atoms ionize,
freed electrons releasing light,
photons of fire to spread

into plasma, hotter temperature,
99.9% of universe that's made
from this fourth matter

that spans and rises
even unto stars and sun
toward galaxies beyond—

releasing solar, stellar winds.

From the Edge of Chaos and Form

II. Electromagnetic Radiation

Fire comes in different colors
from carmine to white (purple
and full spectrum

in between),

this electromagnetic radiation
depending on what's burn-
ing temperature and chemical–

with a little salt for adding too
(if needed for seeing, believing)–
wavelength up, frequency down.

The oxygen and molecules–gas–
heat and fuel, providing punch–
combustion–making it all happen

complete or otherwise–
this time, orange-yellow.

III. The Transfer of Heat

Fire gives the hot for spread
of waves, density differences, molecules from atoms
of there being no stopping what's made to excite,

oxygen along for the journey to lift heat up as needed
when down. Whether solid, liquid, gas, or wave
in space or object, conductible or otherwise,

heat moves in–speed-of-light change.

IV.   The Taming of Ashes

There comes a residue after reaction—
combustion complete
to neither liquid nor gas, this

law of conservation—
from wood to coal—
matter not destroyed—

carbon to be particles
mostly of glass perhaps
or calcium compounds,

but dependent on type—
the what burned and how.

Then to disperse,
become the underground.

Sound, Intention, Word: Moving Waters

Thoughts affect water. Emoto
tested music and prayer,
written words attached
upon a container of ice
crystals,

how responses
changed their structure
from beauty to disarray,
based on positive or negative
sound and vibration,

to find in the end, beginning
awareness: conversation, waters
holding universal language.

Identical Image Not Reflected upon Superimposition

Not superimposable, no mirror image
in chiral molecules, chiral handedness,
stereocenters.

Maybe cosmic rays
to muons magnetically polarized
for two millionths of a second alive

traveling near speed of light
detected more than seven hundred meters
below the earth

dying to electrons' magnetic orientation
always the same, small difference in mutation
rate billions of years ago

the beginnings of life,
in molecules.

Simple, fragility.

From the Edge of Chaos and Form

Waves of Iridescence

Pigmentation and how light travels
as I look at an object of iridescence
in nature's formation of rock, animal, crystal–

hard to believe
the waves of interference
in the light of mysteries

that construct or deconstruct
vibrancy of color
within physical structures

of what's reflected or absorbed outright.

Waves line up *in phase*.
But if Pi-shifted, waves destroy each other
(known also as canceling)
to cause *out of phase* dimming of light.

Troughs and crests beyond my vision
reflect wind waves in air that rush
in washing over me again and again
in what seem like illusions, optical

no sense, yet no doubt particles
that hold a piece of the universe.

Universe of Patterns

Chaos Theory

They say a butterfly can change the world.

In a nonlinear system, mere flapping
can create a critical point for *singularity*
of change beyond the *edge of chaos*.

In *phase space*, nothing stays the same,
no two maps are alike, as in weather
where nothing makes for repetition—

only patterns of wanting to follow
what's known as *strange attractor*,
a favored state with fractal properties
as in snowflakes with self-similarity.

Adding to the mix are *emergence*,
swarm behavior, engineered chaos—

constructed maneuvers for taking control
but still all leading to more change
in a world of dominating non-predictions

within a view of chance, that when looked at
closely make fractal kaleidoscopic patterns.

Between a Star and a Planet

"Failed star," "brown dwarf"–
names that belie your prominence
as if you hadn't been what you are

supposed to be–perfect
in your having enough mass,
enough density and pressure
to keep your core as you want–
without fusion–to cool

on your own timetable
of hundreds of millions of years
in space
to radiate your variances

in your own infrared light.

Supermoon

Directly between Sun and Moon, Earth turns
birthing to blood-red hue a Moon closer
than normal with greens and blues scattered,
refracted, by Earth particles of umbral shadow
to Sun's rays showering
toward total moon eclipse
in wolves howling
coldest time–
early part of the year

Lunar Eclipses

Earth casts blocked-Sun shadow
on Moon in fullness completing orbit.

Three is the number of impact,
the number of eclipse types
and yearly chances of happening.

Total eclipse, blood Moon epithet,
garnering superstitions
of Moon turned red

dependent on dust,
ash, clouds, wavelengths
in red and blue–

optical effects.
Perfect alignment
between Sun/Moon/Earth

isn't always the order.
Moon tilts towards Earth
to inch away yearly
as satellite too far away

to fully fill Earth's demarcation
in umbral shadow

forecasted for change
billions of years from now.

Drifting

From Drifting to Writing in the Rocks: Graptoloids

From early Ordovician you floated
to extinct by Devonian—eras
of your colonizing
continents
before there were fish evolving

to how you took to waves
of seas for rolling through columns
you rose from floor in adjusting form
to become colony, a rhabdosome
around gas-filled membrane

finding purpose in buoyancy
along with nema for attaching
to floating debris, surface
for holding planktonic home, upwelling
exoskeleton of theca cups, many

along branches, first formed
sicula secreted by zooid
from schleroprotein
(like chiton or collagen)
in asexual budding

this animal, first to build
what became stacked and bandaged,
interconnected structure with apertures
for feeding, filtering microplankton
reached by armed tentacles out and around

From the Edge of Chaos and Form

tubes of varying orientations,
surface openings to sophistication,
developing how many animals within
this three-dimensional hanging home
of mobility for maybe swum from—

hermaphroditic animal perhaps—
its habits and life to become predictions,
zooids hundreds of millions of years ago
the changing sea margins altered, land plants
of new growth. Fallings. Joinings, black shale.

Ring of Fire: Eruptions to Earthquakes, Pacific Rim

It started as one:
hundreds of millions of years ago
continent and ocean,

Pangea and Panthalassa
is what there was

before convection currents
took their rolling upper mantle
for breaking the still waking

to plate tectonics of surface
movement floating atop

jockeying for position
in how they scrape, grind,
push each other down, plates,
to the rising of magma

mixing in to separate
and play a part–
explosiveness
through crust, crack
the heat's driving for release

as in

Ring of Fire, famous feared belt–
greatest activity, seismic
for
all sorts–composite mostly,
lava dome, shield, cinder cone–
volcanos all–and plateaus (lava), plugs

From the Edge of Chaos and Form

calderas and tuffs, pyroclasts
as reminders like vents and fissures,
melting of ice, back arc and basin,
trenches and hot spots, more rainfall,

the tuff and the tephra, clouds of ash,
gasses, tropical cyclone low pressures,
Pacific Ocean rim–main plate the Pacific,
fastest-moving changer over dense
ocean plates to melt through subduction

in creating eruptions 40,000 kilometers
long this chain of friction unknown time period
lithosphere of action when is it coming
another time around of Earth's core
changing in flows of iron, cooling now faster.

Da Ow Aga: Edge of Lake Tahoe, Phrase of the Washoe Tribe

Fault blocks up-thrown,
Ice Age moved down

Glaciers through canyons, west side,
Moraines left behind

Till lava flow, north side,
Mt. Pluto formed dam across
River outlet
Before water erosion of path;

Snowfall, streams, runoff
To fill one of deepest
Lakes, alpine freshness
Surrounded by cedar and pine,

Fir and shrub,
Evergreen groundcover and brush,

Willow, lupine, phlox, penstemon
Wyethia, lily, and paintbrush,

So many flowers to name
Making home with the lake
Of the hidden fish

In the shades of blue
Vibrating in molecules, shortest wavelengths
Visible into indigo

Waters where I breathe and live at the edge
On volcanic rock

Once cooled above, cooled below.

From the Edge of Chaos and Form

dewdíʔiš Lísiʔ, déʔek degót'aʔa–
Between the trees,
Broken, split rock.

Gaps in Canopy: Tree Crown Decisiveness

They call it shyness,
the scientists do. I call it

plants knowing all along
how to make the most of light

and share their floors of forest.
They go about their business

of loving what they have
making the most of opportunity.

Optimizing light exposure
is what it's called, is one theory,

along with sharing communally.
Gaps in canopy allow for forest floor

and animals to benefit
while increasing photosynthesis.

Maybe, too, the trees,
lessen exposure to disease

by keeping their distance,
preventing the spread of pain.

Whatever all the reasons,
trees use their phytochromes

to find the sun and keep
from scraping others.

They thrive on diversity.
They know how to get along.

From the Edge of Chaos and Form

Achene with Wings

It's called the wingnut, the helicopter,
the whirligig, that little samara
autorotating down for the ground

as one-seeded dried fruit
that spins from the tree
to be dispersed by wind.

It made it past dormancy
for release to fall to germinate
to environmental whims–

taking a hold of all of us.

Stolon: Plant Extension

They call you runner,
stem reaching for light,
adventitious bud in the crown zone,
roots and shoots rising from nodes.

You are storer of food,
propagator in your own right,
horizontal spreader along the ground
as you slink and arch

toward
welcoming branch
for water, soil, nutrients

and star–
most distant neighbor–
your sun, with light arriving
whole through dark

roads along the casting ways
of Orion's beaming arm.

Dandelion

It's your parachute that takes you away,
the one of old age that disperses your seed,

when bracts bend down for launching
your release to the dropping of stamens,

dried petals, the adjustment of air
to moisture timing just right.

You've gone from bright yellow
ray floret to white hair brittle

dome of stars.
I love you, flower dandelion

(epithet ruderal).

Night-Blooming Cereus

The moon guides you,
in fullness drawing
your one single blooming
fragrant opening
this one time only–
yearly when hawkmoth
will find you
for pollinating
from anther to stigma
within dangling filaments
of shooting stars fallen
from cumulonimbus
appearance
bordered by sunrays
bursting from
quiet organza-like
ruffled hood of whiteness
opening sky, Earth,
to stalk, to stem,
for what's to come
of this bearing luscious,
colorful, this
leathery eventual,
spiked fruit–
perfection's dragon.

From the Edge of Chaos and Form

Glowing Mushroom

The secret's in bioluminescence,
where at night in the Brazilian coconut forest
foxfire comes alive, the blue glow

attracting lovers of scent and sight—

Lucifer, bringer of light,
summoned into molecule
of luciferin and enzyme
for lighting up the night—

to reactions
of oxygen and energy
activating electron state

to when—
excitement dies down—
and the light turns on

inside forest full

of pale, cool mushrooms.

Honey Mushroom, Blue Mountains

Honey mushroom, largest organism
visible in autumn after first rains
four square miles
from thousands of years
Blue Mountains

rooting in Oregon,
base of trees, fruiting forest

from black shoestring-
like rhizomorphs
between bark, tissue,
and on root systems

comprising hyphae
filaments, labyrinth
of leaking enzymes

for extending territory
under/over ground
in genetically same

gigantic form quietly

ever so quietly
one by one
taking trees down.

Sulphur Shelf on Western Hemlock

The wound is of the heartwood
where rot works its way in

from outer mushroom, parasitic
in its orange-yellow brightness
of body, soft and moist, planar
gibbous moon-shaped folds of ruffle

fungi flesh absorbing carbohydrates
how hatchet marks once struck

into becoming darkening wood,
blades of no pitch to cover
softening to what can't be fought–

to another
sustenance in decay, another's loss,

a tree still holding on
to remnants, impermanent
joinings,

this earth.

Redroot

Bees ignore, ants adore
your no nectar, fleshy appendages
by seeds to offer. Rich coating elaiosome.
Hermaphroditic, self-pollinating.
Toxic yet medicinal and dye providing.
In loamy fertile soils, rhyzomes colonize.
Woodland poppy family
growth hereby welcomed.

In Motion

Animal: Living Soul

Hebrew scripture, Genesis:
Chapters One and Two.

Animal beings, translated:
living souls, *nefesh chaya*,

life force with divine breath
blessed with *ruach*, spirit of God,

will and consciousness.

We have gardens to tend:
abad and shamar,

to serve and
exercise great care over

as we are one
body sharing this Earth

needing protection, eager for love.

Congregation

Golden currant bush
boasts berries orange enough
for robins to open wide their beaks
enough to take in juiciness
and fatten breasts to puff out
pleased. Do stay a while plumped
within autumn's leaved branches
hosting delicious morning's feast.
Round of robins I've never seen
such as this one ornamenting bush.
Aves, do come back again, please!
Fill yourselves with nourishment.
Keep swilling sun star wishes!

Return of the Doves

Tree at end of spring,
chosen home for courting doves
under canopy of branches coo

and rub, caress
from head to neck
and preen themselves
each other softly too

in nestling far from calls
that jar, their world a birth
for what is right

in two eggs—days to come—
necessary warmth,
parents who take their turns

at love at love at love.
They build their nest,
they watch and wait.

Skies and clouds reflect
scatterings of light
flutterings of breath

in dives, departures,
protections for instinct,
milk joinings beak to beak

eyes for guiding, wing to wing,
step for step,
the sight of what's beyond

From the Edge of Chaos and Form

spruce holding belief
adding the bloom, what space
the boughs to catch

the touch, the wonder
along bark and needles–

others' *singing* life.

California Quail: Covey at Old Doves' Nest

With the falling of snow
in the solstice of winter,
quail rise to their roost,

a covey under branches,
the protection of spruce

that lets winged visitors in
to feel its bark,
to join with dormancy

as the world slows down

as the tree becomes harbor–

needle wax resisting freeze,

sugar, protein,
calcium, hormones,
outer bark air pockets,
insulation as needed–

ways all to regulate
formations of icy glass,
pitch to transfer nutrients–

reaching for life–
standing for warmth
as the tree faces its winter
and the quail take to season

From the Edge of Chaos and Form

for the shelter they all hold
together, sentinels watchful
of movements treading close
to family at feathery rest
huddled in avian line,

their facing another branch

like extensions of heartwood
hidden, heart to radiate

emphasis in the middle,
the very sound,
the birds' call,

the amphibrach,
poetic foot of telling

of movement, coming or current,
or even

proclaiming separation.

Changing of Light, Losses in Song

2014 report: 421 million birds gone—last thirty years—Europe
2019 study: Three billion birds disappeared—last fifty years—North America
One quarter missing—last three decades—Lake Constance—birds of Switzerland, Germany

Shrinking baseline syndrome.
Major loss across all biomes.
At risk for extinction—one million plants and animals.

Potential system collapse—warning.
Birds as augury—barometer of sky and earth,
migrations dropping in numbers, bird size, wing length.

Rainforests eradicated, areas of Earth converted.
Loss of natural land, habitats for bird. Even in darkness
celestial cues lost. Circadian rhythms disrupted.

Energy wasted. Artificial light at night
disorients. More vocalization, fatal collisions—
buildings, pylons, posts, and fences,

wires, ground, and signs to blame, lights distracting, birds

we are and will be
missing.

Straw-Colored Fruit Bats' Path of Endangerment: South Africa, Kasanka National Park

From the tropical Congo jungles
to Zambia's Kasanka National Park
at the time of first rains ripening
for patch of evergreen swamp forest

hot-dry for flying-in fruit-bat swarms
dappling skies for thousands of kilometers
—ten million in number—megacolony
of largest mammal migration—flying foxes

coming to desires for waterberry,
banana, agave, fig, mango, masuku
in mushito forest of red mahogany, red
milkwood, cinchona—from West Africa

more of bats arriving for pulp, juice,
abundance by the waters, Musola River,
to land for roosts, their days, the camps,
cloaks closed, upside down hanging, warm,

or fanning on branches, or moving about
waiting for sunup, sundown, falling into
bustle for meeting with night, the flight
with moon for watching over scented—

each pup hanging on to mother, hunger driving
what's turning—agriculture—adding
plant for wind—turbines planning—developers
snatching for land—fires by poachers—motives

upwards 300,000 forest hectares disappearing
—biodiversity for destroying—
yearly to Zambia's designs with new money
moving to farm maize, soya, wheat commodities

and wind-energy center to build, grow in line
proposed towers on path of bats in flight,
fateful through park over savannah, wetlands,
floodplains, shrubland and forest, over Africa

stretches of what are losing to dreamers
taking down trees, the hunting of creatures
dispersing the seeds, reforesting, cycles of growth
needed for pollinations vital for ecosystems—

animals of endangered species, overlooked
falling into shutdown, no food, less room, forced

way to desertification, habitat loss, attackers to face—
all closing in—blades for removal—scarrings—Earth

From the Edge of Chaos and Form

In Honor of Sloths

Who said you are Sin—
that mortal kind—
clinging to cecopria tree?

You are not human—
have nothing to do
with Evagrius, ascetic

of the third century—
no, you go way beyond
to 35 million years ago

megatherium you were called,
six-metric-ton body roaming
through forests, savannahs to

how could they fault you
for their own human waywardness,
as in Chaucer, Dante,

Saint Thomas Aquinas,
who equated you with
human vapidness,

lack of feeling, so-called
dulling of spiritual progress,
some kind of failure

as if you're not doing
what you're supposed to,
as if you're lacking, shirking,

wasting time when what it is
is your loving trees, rainforest,
eating of leaves

glorifying sun above humans'
cultivation of coca plant
to fuel greed—their cocaine

habit rising to take you down
to—you do everything right

before humans
misattribute sin.

From the Edge of Chaos and Form

What About the Cockroach

Cockroach—
not the sort of topic
people clamor to talk about
in this time of climate crisis,

like how fast roaches can run
when they see you—
like two hundred miles per hour for snap getaways—
or how they can stay forty-five minutes under water

or live without heads if they have to
for days, with their separate head and second brain
staying alive, too; and the same goes for food and water—
roaches being able to go without for long periods of time.

Then there are the roaches holding their breath
when needed—for seven whole minutes, in fact—
or their slowed-down breathing through their sides
(called spiracles), survival tactic for drier times.

And they don't care too much about what they eat—
barring cucumbers—such as toenails, glue, dead things
and whatnot; they pick up after us dirty humans, after all,
and they do pollinate flowers, about a dozen species or so.

And if you're not more than 900 times their weight
stomping down upon them, they will survive the crush
for they are excellent acrobats in the flattening department
and will survive extreme conditions—arctic, desert, tropical.

And did you know they fight off toxins
all from an enzyme making them resistant
to chemicals and poisons aimed at killing them off?
Their bodies adjust, such as to radiation also,

from a nuclear explosion, or adjust to the sweet baits
that make them change receptor hairs for taste
to make the laced glucose bitter so as to keep safe.
And they are most social in their choosing democratic

ways of life to protect the collective.
And what about how females can forego a mate–
their parthenogenetic way of giving birth when needed.
No wonder close to five thousand species survive

of this incredible bug that outsmarts us human creatures
time and time again in spite of how we kill their earth
and warm their temperatures, messing with all ecosystems,
which only will make roaches smartly take more to the skies.

Snowshoe Hare at Sunrise, Sunset

Under the canopy of fallen trees
when snow meets daylight
and the quiet of mountainside,

the snowshoe hare crouches to
wait in the coldness of white,
for light to take shape

after the changing of coat
in the shortening of days
in droplets to form ice

all-around crackles to break
for the hare to take hold
of branches in late winter's feast.

Cystisoma, Marine Crustacean

In the twilight zone of muscle and outer shell,
ocean home of incident light

in the deepest blue to black
with retinas extended over surface of head,

visual pigment of red
your sheets of eyes looking up

for finding shadows,
your prey, their trying to hide

in bioluminescence
or flashing-of-light

predators not to disguise–
all of you this moment

in the darkness downwellings
to move, maybe like you–

invisible–bacteria nanoplankton
as coating for anti-reflection,

protuberances on cuticle
evenly spaced for tapering

From the Edge of Chaos and Form

(on legs, carapace)
for reducing reflections

as in just the wrong curling
or tilting altering polarization

or maybe the brood patch, visible–
might just give you away.

School of Fish

You are parts to a whole,
swimming unending rhymes
to hold on to unity
in the clearest of blue.

You fall, you dive, you rise
turning the obligate
together in moves
complex and polarized.

Working as one,
you know lateral lines,
sensing all zones,
vortexes drawing you in

to alignment that's yours,
repulsions not long,
you are like shooting stars
in the deep swimming on.

Seahorse Birthing

Exploding brood patch
hole opens contractions

another fry to spill like stars
shooting towards oblivion
in billowing waters
with maybe five only
of one thousand surviving
babies delivered to forces
ready to be encapsulated

before fatigue settles the father,
hardworking seahorse
drifting down after birthing,

his sinking into twilight zone…

before the next dance begins,
perhaps that evening
as female seahorses hover, eager
in offering him their seahorse eggs
to be fertilized and carried.

He impresses with his pouch so big.
The females take notice and float around
in competition, hoping to be picked.

With whose tail will he entwine?
Whose plate colors will change with his?
For days they will swim in courtship.

It seems the chosen one he rises with
to the ocean surface days later
tenders him the brightness, the eggs

he'll hold and oxygenate, salinate,

until another cycle

in his continual seahorse pregnancies
resumes.

From the Edge of Chaos and Form

Male Gentoo Penguin: Preparation for Incubation

What you need are pebbles–
more–hard to find–
on Antarctica Peninsula–
and a spot for building your nest with
expectant mate. You found the right
smooth stone for wooing her
as you bowed your head
before trumpeting skyward.
She took your token and waited,
bided her time. Now you return
with another gift and then another
in an afternoon start
of perfect pebble offerings.

Mollusk Migration

Family of Neritidae, snails of freshwater
(amphidromous) settle at river mouth as juveniles
after larval stage of swept downstream to sea.

They wait for rides through tropical scenery, up slopes
on the back sides of subadults, snails who carry them
perhaps as far as ten kilometers in a couple years' time.

On their way home again, maybe to same spot as their birth,
young travelers land, dismount, and leave their final marks
as two concentric levels in shells of their most kind hosts.

To remain in paradise is their choice, happy upon tufa beds,
gorging on micro food, algae of deliciousness,
as the spray from waterfalls covers them rainbow moist.

Dragonfly Migration

She holds her shell, chiton
armor that once protected her
till now she's emerged
from nymph stage
with new skin,
compound eyes
to see the world
above lake water
where she's lived
and scavenged for food.
She must fly now,
make a maiden voyage.
Wing-whirring. Warming.
Rain slips off her wings:
lotus effect
self-cleaning, drying.
Species unknown–ancestry
320 million years before her time–
as she heads for ancient ocean
waters in fullness of colors
flying to all reaches
waves of endlessly rolling

Tarantula Migration

Over arid land and short prairie grass,
the tarantula shares its burrow
with narrow-mouthed toad
who keeps away the ants

and will protect spider eggs
that come this time of year,
after late August to October
when the spider males surface

to make their trek, maybe a mile,
in search of females accepting–
or not, of suitor tap at her silky door–
risking their lives after molt, how

males crawl through shadows and light,
vibration and motion, hairs detecting
the feel of chemical, wind, and many cues
much of their bodies for picking up–much like

whether or not their wooed one taps back
and lets them in, or comes outside to greet
their earnestness in this one chance–time of their life
to play the dance that only she's expected to outlive.

Interspecies Interacting

Forging the Distance

I like how the bear steers clear
in its path up the hill
through snow
deep
through the trees

to where it joins with winter
in shutting down
to the faster pace of life without–

when it can draw on itself
inner resources to be still

and to wait and sleep,

enjoy its snow cave,

as the rest of the world
takes its steps perhaps into

trying to be something,
trying to move ahead

as if owning

mystery.

Family Summit Wanderings

My mother and I walk east
midafternoon, mountain meadow,
early fall. Willows and lodgepole,
jeffrey pine, parsnip, rosy everlasting,
golden weeds drying brittle.

Out of not expecting–
new umber color
movement–
animal back side

among woody greens and yellows–
a bear cub–

turns and runs north in a burst
of how I catch the profile
of surging–another adult bear
following as if to play,

offspring the trees are hiding
before bears moving our way–

one cub leading the mother,
basin's dirt road above.

My dog companion
picking up scent,
ready to investigate

as we turn back
to revisit

amber meadow's
presumed place of safety

below where Ursidae roams
with desires—and everything wild.

From the Edge of Chaos and Form

Intimations of Bobcat

I know you are close

fur soft, providing warmth

I could follow you
till our eyes met

and yet know better
not to bother

but to leave you quietly
to your natural world

I think of
you in cold-air wildness
among boulders
inside logs under ledges
in thickets for cover

striding across mountain slope

having your shelters

spread out for nights
and days no other place,
but rather

I am watching these trails

right here how long
this everything right,
hallowed ground–

awakening.

Landscape for Limitations

Coyote takes the risk
of staying close to human
indoors joined to food source
in colder days of winter,

February's mating season,
storms before another, an alpha
male presumably,
approaches for warning—

which is when fast fly
the corners of this one
battle intense for territories
prolonging show of power—

rivalry uncontested
for one who must lower—
belly to ground, head tucked—
no howl to find what little cover
protects under bare branches

food not plentiful, and
pups to come in spring den
with need to be fed,

as some will one day
leave their pack, like this one
coyote's choosing—

future, alone.

The Wake Capture

I am butterfly
        emerging chrysalis

Earthbound nourished
        joined to night and leaves
                holding open

Born for flight
        sensing—eyes, touch,
                antennas, ultraviolet guiding

Wings
        of figure-eight motion
                uplift

To clapping
        air of acceptance
                I am the vortex, colors passing,

Known effects
        softly powdered, nectar my center,
                I am winds shaping
                        worlds

Dear Killer

Taking Down the Bull

Dear Matador,

What do you do with the ear?
What do you do with that horse,
one of yours used by a picador,
the horse whose ears you stuffed,
blocked the sounds from entering
with newspaper wet for crushed?

And what of the horse's blindfold,
your keeping from sight
that prepping of the bull,
those lances driving into muscle
and back the twisting and gouging
to spill out blood it is just getting started

and the horse's cord
vocally cut, so no one would hear the screams.
What of that horse who wanted to run,
who would have run from ring
when taunting began

when weight had already been tied
down on bull's neck for weeks the beatings,
filed-down horns, petroleum jelly eyes,
agitation increasing without food or water
in small isolation cell, the salt, laxatives,
drugs to tranquilize, harpoon to minimize–

you can't have the bull be too strong–

which is where the banderilleros come in,
the ones who go on stabbing and waving flags
to tire the bull to dizzy the maddening
of no stopping maniacal barbarism.

From the Edge of Chaos and Form

Which is where you come in
with your something to prove
sword or dagger, cutting spinal cord
or aorta is what you're after.
Final blow the crowd happy with.

Hence, the ear you won, the ear severed
as trophy of your having the advantage,

in the way you'll drive July bulls to sea,
The Bous a la Mar, the Toro de Jubilo,
where you'll set horns on macabre fire.

Dear Matador,
What makes you think this all some sport?
In the end, to me, you always lose your heart.

Perception Ablation

We take away her navigation,
polarized light, vision impacted
through disorientation, her rubbing
the place of injury, not searching
for shelter, tail flicking
as escape reflex
stress hormone release

at eye removal—

pinching or ligation,
cauterization or blade slitting—
whichever method used
for making shrimp mass produce
within ponds made for crowding
dirtiest of carbon footprint
on razed mangrove forestlands

moved from deep-sea trawling
floors of coral reef and seagrass,
marine mammals, seabirds, fish,
turtles, shark, octopus, crab,
sea snake, starfish, sea horse
caught in nets forming "trash fish"

to die or be turned overboard,
maybe crushed on deck, maybe
later turned to mash as feed

From the Edge of Chaos and Form

the peoples are slaving, dying for
promises of cash for flow the jobs
to sustain is a lie it's a crime
they'll be taken away to maybe
shot execution-style onboard
if trying to free themselves
or in asking for something more

than a ship or a shed no escape from
no wages, bondage stolen benefit
being led by security signing off
on conveyor belt washing out
to sea and not–

shrimp alive the deheadings–

show losses, removals of every kind
signs everywhere dropping off
wastes of our reminding pollution

Stolen Property: Goosebumps from "Diamond Area"

Also known as "crown,"
back side of Ostrich
large quills
pulled
follicles torn
increase in value
scars, goosebumps
show off
purses and wallets
the short life
incubated
cracked to "cashed"
no parents for caring
dirt pens of crowding
sack over head
blinding
leg restraints
clipping of wings
feathers and plumes
to dusters to shoes
belts and costumes
Mardi Gras
Moulin Rouge
runways for fashion
you're everywhere
remnants
around the world
kicked
body-face punched
laughed at looks
not able to dance
no mornings your twirls
uplifting of wings
the happy of wild

From the Edge of Chaos and Form

gone to upholstery,
production of belts,
luggage and gloves,
sporting goods sold
not to forget
it all sounds so good
as you slip on the floor
having seen death ahead
no flight without time
or voice to behold
just stun and then knife
a struggle, then hung

The Shearing Floor

Comfort shorn to beatings on the floor
of twisted necks, scrotum, testicles,
an ear taken off after tails, to urine that spreads
how I can see they think you're just the wool
of chokes to knee to chest,
no time their time
punches thrown to kicks
breaking poked to blind
faces thrown to pushed
sheep to chute
doesn't matter the bleeds,
their time to focus on–these humans–
their needs for slamming
words with down I won't repeat,
as if you're the ones wrong and yet
their own mistakes for covering up
to sew right then and there
cuts they've popped the organs out
for shaming further pains
while blaming their own misfortunes
on struggles of your will to fight
not of your choosing being left in
overcrowded pens you are the wool again
virtues dragged, gone for invention's sake
from chunks of skinned-off knife
side back warding off flystrikes
that will come still
that will find terror in their hosts, physical loss
forming seeds for life to feed off yet another
and yet another of human errors making off
again these signs, this time, this way,
these hosts and parasite.

Reptilian People

You carry the death
of three crocodiles—
or alligators are they?
in that bag of
what does it matter
manufacturer—yours
of skinned alive
for Hermès
fashion designer
garnering 43,000—
or was it more than
400,000 dollars?—Birkin
diamond and gold
Himalayan style
most expensive
handbag all the way
from Padenga
or Lone Star—
or was it Georgia?
for Prada? Vietnam?
Louis Vuitton?
in dank pits of darkness
for no room
the tanks on another farm
to be built there's talk
for 50,000 Australian
crocs, this one prison
to hold—to force down
plunger through
head, spine to tail
body all tightly held

rod for pithing
ramming brain,
add the sawing
of neck, stabbing
of vertebrae (cervical),
of no escaping losses
bleeding out can take time
for belly-makings of design
in multibillion-dollar industry
being able to say
killer label holds
in your hands the price
of what never had life.

From the Edge of Chaos and Form

Pangolin Endangerment

Most widely trafficked mammal
yet seemingly unknown, you, pangolin,
creature of solitariness in your habitat
of erasures toward ecological disaster

of human creation that kills for paste
kills for powders of your scales
(keratin made, like in human nails
of nothing more than protein

that helps form cells) and yet
scales are stolen for cures,
fetuses for soup, humans
consuming sufferings:

their own wounds,
words, epilepsy, poison,
pains, witchery, attacks
in need of protections,
rituals, lactation, fertility,
and on this list goes

to how you are a delicacy
proving people false richness
in your non-existent luxury
of their invoking your magic
from your other world, yours–

the trees, the burrows,
your roundness forming
to closing out hostile forces
you could roll from edges,
holding the earth as you go.

From the Edge of Chaos and Form

Animal: Live Transport Airborne

If I could hand you freedom, love
suspending what there's nothing more I can give

than your vision of cloud and sky unfurling
this moment in pieces that you fall with
first dangling free-board hull-side

lifting sicknesses, mechanical crane meeting,
your dragged by bound leg, letting go you are
infirm ripped from the downing of thousands

upon thousands, *your* kind, your creatureliness
in cargo ship of unfitness carrying destinations
terminal, to nothing to normal this back and forth

crowding to shortening
days to another storm rising, starving,
your thirst, disabusing not
of waters reflecting comforts,
constant in their letting go, oceans' washings,
no mercies

there, as if I could hold you
in the light of nothing holding on
in the light of nothing holding *us* together.

Battery Cage in Blackout House

Ten to a cell (2 by 1½ feet),
                Hens

forced molting, reduced light,
absent water/feed, freshness to breathe

missed sun, flaming earth not to feel
cracked bones, diseases, disorders
        (rotting eggs in oviduct,
        large eggs internally stuck,
        uterine prolapse) perhaps

infections expected can't forget
skeletal paralysis commonplace
dismissed in stepped upon

to spread no wings–7 billion male chicks–
7 billion male chicks discarded yearly–
              not to forget
       (gassed, macerated, decapitated)

multi-billion dollar egg-unfertilized business

of hens maybe given two years
of suffocated–oh, and not to forget
expected, same means of death
(one more method remembered)

of literal suffocations–male chicks.

Artificial Insemination: Dairy Goat Method

Like Medieval torture rack
elongating bodies to the point of break,
you are clamped down, splayed,
flipped on your back,
head tilted down,
acute angle, the body
of silence not to move
nor consent—
insertion of hormone,
insertion of semen,
(progesterone sponge
having been removed
vaginally). And—
 there you go!
Simple! Release, quick!
Pulled off to slap floor
(off your dolly of sorts),
you're ready to be moved
like a sack of brown rice
not in its right place yet,
not in the order of things,
not in the next right line
you need to be going in
on conveyor belt line
for the making of milk,
for the boxing up of gifts,
another package of sorts
with its rips and spills
that will happen to you
that will empty to fill
that will shuttle you through
mishandlings all
of beauty forsaken,
trapped—not visible.

Elegy for the Horses

1.
Bidders come—
saleyards flood—
horse whip flogs—
reminiscent of—
Blacks sold off—
branded, tarred—
jammed in pens—
poked and prodded—
auctioned off—
18th-19th century—
not so long ago—

2. Racehorses:
Rebel Prince, Perfectly Spun,
Startreusse, Courtney's Luv,

National Flag, Touchdown Miss,
Explore the World, Halo's Image,
Millster, Cloverdale, Unbuckled—

names of the pedigreed (just some)
unharnessed unto blood.

3. Knackeries win
purebred, standardbred, quarterbred, Arabian,
thoroughbred, feral doesn't matter when
doesn't matter how taken to consumption
or cut up filled with swarming maggots
cracked as bones in vats of refuse.

4.
"Please pass the butter," she says
at dining table of lace and linen cloth
in her birdcage veil hat with feather
sticking up like her in her tie-neck dress
of blue and yellow floral patterns.

The man across from her, seated
corpulent, handlebar mustache,
in sharkskin suit with leather buckle shoes
sets down his sterling silverware–too hard

upon Bone china delicate from cattle ash
and eyes his quail and crusty bread,
swirls the red Bordeaux within its glass
and forgets about–never built a bond

with horses he just sold,
ones who brought no profits.

"At the track–we'll go again,"
he says, "I know I'll win–win most big,"
and pats the beads of sweat upon his brow.

The woman nods her head, dabs her lips
with napkin lifted from her lap.

Man squints at watch fob from his vest.
Tucks the piece back upon his breast.

Myth and Artifact

Celestial Wakenings: Vincent van Gogh's *The Starry Night*

"We take death to reach a star"–
more than religion to the afterlife,
where we might land on other hemisphere.

Cypress are the trees of death.
Church steeple reaching sky.
Yellow will never leave my heart.

Impasto, squeezing, brings me close.
Does not matter the moon.
Stylized I will not dismiss.

The swirl of wind turns me round.
Mistral strong and cold
slants my light, down

behind bars. I cannot paint upstairs,
but Venus I see from everywhere.
Spirals and comet show my way.

Galaxy of whirlpool, Rosse and Parsons,
Flammarion proven. I am meant to spin,
led to find. "Hope is in the stars."

From the Edge of Chaos and Form

Birth of Venus as Painted by Botticelli

Everything is floating

Hora, minor goddess of spring.
Island of Cyprus, rose petals
to laurel trees
to giant shell holding
fair-skinned Love,

covering what Aura and Zephyr
might blow to expose
to nakedness as wrong
in times
when Plato projected
divine love
as more than the physical

that's not for lasting, here depicted
as one race flowing of hair and youth

as Cronus overthrew
father, Uranus–parts thrown to the sea

thereupon birthing
full-grown Venus
emerging from foam, cool spray.

Meeting the Lion and Gypsy in Henri Rousseau's Image in the Sand

The lion spotted me. There were no trees.
The gypsy, smiling, slept on, mandolin at her side.
How far had she traveled? I wondered,
and her jug half full, the still lake
behind her joining with mountains
and starry moonlit sky.

I too was wandering with the quiet
night when this lion lay down,
in what looked like worn earth
where it must have made its bed
a long time, maybe waiting for the woman
to wake, for her to take up her staff,
brush herself off and head to dreams
with the lion following,

the lion sometimes licking at her feet,
sometimes sweeping across her side.

From the Edge of Chaos and Form

Autumn Mourning[1]

The last image of my lover's body,
the swirling of her hair and back
and longing, her curving into light

how I touched us into her holding
and feeling taking back
how she could not bear for life

in her brokenness not for opening
chignon high on head, neck of grace
unraveling the strokes of my coddling

not enough or too much
to be overbearing
her looking away

to the past replaying
before us theatrics
of entrapment in remembrance

moments of lasting
impression leading
her descending, another fall

to the ground of our winter
of her Hades below bedrock
opening chasm

no turning back
the falling deeper
to flowers folding

darkness to wither
of stained by seed of fruit,
pomegranate. Persephone.
Our love. Unknown. Hidden.

---

[1] September equinox when the Greek Goddess Persephone annually returned to the underworld.

Medusa: Demystifying Myth

I'm known as head of snakes,
woman betrayed, woman with tusks,
beard, forsaken. No mistaking
how I stare you into stone,

engender fear, as I've lived
as priestess of temple
never to call my own.
What story there is of beauty

is mere legend. And Poseidon
never owned me. I fought back
to where no man has wanted
my stare, my touch, body of damage.

Athena's curse struck to last.
Then my head I lost to Perseus,
again used on shield to scare with force.
Snakes squirm. Neck birthed

boar and horse.
I've nothing left
to die for.

In the Labyrinth of Minotaur

I was the sacrifice, the second cycle
of seven years' time crossing by ship
to Crete over sea to face the labyrinth,
to meet the minotaur, man
with head of bull (son of Pasiphae) lost
to the underground alone
to wander, to feed on darkness
and loneliness of tunnels
with no Daedalus to find, no fix,
no comfort, no guide,
but the soft skin of woman
he has been without–how I drift
to some other place, my Athens
with its light, no teeth upon me,
no bloodthirsty tongue
as I turn to stone,
given up. Minos, King
seeking vengeance
for lost son, I am
daughter lost to kin,
no ending
for youth betrayed,
sounds of randomness.
With innocence, tears,
I go down.

From the Edge of Chaos and Form

Pipe Bowl: Plains Indian, Cheyenne, Artist Unknown

Whose hands has this passed through,
pipe bowl, calumet as stem once joined
perhaps, male to female to form creation,
sacred pipe of different purposes.

Catlinite, iron-rich claystone
beneath groundwater level
between Sioux Quartzite layers,
rapid to erode to elements above,

only hand tools used for its long
unearthing from mudrock, like tobacco
gathered, stems and blossoms,
harvested by hand, dried and oiled

as offering to spirits, sky and earth,
at times for peace, the Sun Dance,
the sealing of agreements, protections
needed for expeditions, war,

ceremony, establishing of alliances.
Whose hands carried and held
tobacco ties, pipe bag, pipe bowl
hard minerals or sandstone,

grit and animal hide, bow for shaping,
polishing with water and fat,
sacred the alliances, this herb,
this stone, this flesh of oneness.

Disc to Disbeliefs

Anything great adds to mystery, as in
Nebra Star (or Sky) Disc of Bronze Age,
Unetice culture, Germany, forestland
of controversy in answers, definitions,
meanings for not solved in what this is

in how precise arc degrees at sides of disc
(each 82° of circle) sunrise-sunset solstices
angle of winter-summer Mittelburg,
moon phase calculated,
location of stars arrived at

Pleiades prominent
as sun traveled the sky in solar boat
to disappear to the underworld
every night at the darkness of right
before the agriculture by day, the equinox

of autumn and spring predictions,
the trades, of gold and tin from Cornwall,
copper from Swiss Alps five hundred meters
down in earth to the question of tools, hoard
of unmatchables, some say the moves,

the size, the signs of Iron Age–
strangeness in the find, looters with lies
to brokenness, burial among barrows outside–
enclosure, uncovered as something more–
than believed in.

Bad Directions: Ptolemy's Crowning Delayed
(Interpretation of Crowson's "Diaphona" Collage)

Urania follows coordinates,
intending to crown Ptolemy,

whose map has lost her
to the Pacific Ocean

in the middle of jellyfish
she has never seen before

as she thinks of Doric columns
between which he waits on step

for his honoring, stone platform
behind, on which Syrus will stand

for bestowing rod of astronomy
before fellow countrymen throng.

Yet it remains mere dream
as Urania's chariot veers

off course from heavens
in round-the-globe trip

to fatigue, her sleep of stag
in 18th century gown, REM's

futuristic deer who directs her
by pointing: Egypt–there.

Earth center. Her eyes open.

Liminal Spaces

Boxes in Transit

I am shuffle
I am wanting
Open to find me
Laying mixed with layers
Jumble of words,
Trinkets of sound
Shake and some rattle
Sides of cardboard, pop,
That can rip, be punctured
I am all loose and structured
So many, these boxes
Tumbled going somewhere
Going everywhere
Delivering chaos,
Contents,
Memories and home
To never again
Be, from emptying, the same

Motel Room Denied

No room for rent
to the homeless man
wanting in from the cold

he's been out too long in
and could die from by next storm.

Money he scrounged
should cover the night–
he knows that as fact,
he begged long for
certain amount.

Receptionist raises the price.
More cash than he has.

She wants him gone–
no mess, no problem.

No foreign species allowed.

PTSD: Distancings

Toddler cries. Doll is lost.
Dirty diapers, splattered bib.

Yard of garbage and scrap metals.
Dog scratches at door to be let in,
also fed. Gnaws at sores on legs.

Snow starting to fall
to shivering boniness
in man and dog,
this young shirtless parent
not having slept or bathed
going on three days now
can't remember now

as he forces drug deal
over landline
from run-down rental
behind now two months in payment.

Girlfriend gone. County jail
five more weeks likely.

Old Chevy Chevelle
dead to driveway
no escape in
waiting engine's replacement.

Young man can't go back
to the missed, to
all what could have happened,
what did and didn't,
never should have been in the family,
back of mind

From the Edge of Chaos and Form

rending marks that stain as seeping blood

widening on altar cloth of whiteness.

A Leg, a Coat, a Hat, a Bark of Lost Dog Left

A leg, a coat, a hat,
a bark of lost dog left
in war zone, persons down,
bound, shot, midday
walk about,

walk the dog,
buy the bread, phone a friend.
Climb a tree, pedal a bike.

Clouds drift by,
siren alarms, fire flares up,
no snores are heard,
no laughter,
no meaning

for a soldier able to kill
rape to laugh–

smile like he would with son
or daughter, grandmother
grandfather,

elderly pair reading a newspaper,
removing their slippers,

tucking themselves in for
one more cozy night ahead.

From the Edge of Chaos and Form

A leg, a coat, a hat,
a bark of lost dog left.

A girl in nightgown
wanders out, blood
on forehead. Another
mortar blast.

Mother, father
lost to missions, the unrest.

Tomorrow another day
spilling out. Whatever's left.

"Reform": Native American Identity

Pulled from family
and forced into boarding school
that spoke another language
far from what I knew
to learn Christianity
that as a Native American "savage"
child they called me to convert
in school a uniform to wear
my hair cut short
to be like them,
white people
I knew nothing of.
Lost reason,
heritage, my people.
I tried to run.
Got dragged back—ordered
to hard labor outside
with no food. Busted
open my head, they did
to teach me a lesson.
Beat me again and again for my escape
and lied about what had happened.
There never was any love,
not in what they did, not in what they said.
I've hated white people ever since.
I'll run whenever I can.

Definitions: Beautiful

I am not what you'd call beautiful.
I've no white skin or blonde hair
the way that I'd want,
no long legs or big breasts
or straight teeth or slim hips to waist.

I'm just a girl in shabby clothes
who wonders when I'll eat again

or bathe or go to the schoolroom I skip
out of repeatedly. I'm on the run now third time

from home and from myself over and over—
girl overlooked—

the one who can't stand to see herself,
who avoids mirrors or talking outright,

needing to shun people as much as possible.
I want to fade like water sucked up dry
in the cracking desert sands that I see in pictures.

How I want to fade like sun at day's end
or like a life grown old that waits for ashes.
I want to disappear now, knowing

no one will understand my need to
just be myself and to be glad. To revel in that.

That, *that* would be my definition of beautiful.

The Unsilencing

1
raped—my wife our unborn child—captain—
crewmen watched from foredeck—joked

cannot kill cannot cannot do my body spooning
a brother im forced to lie against as another spoons me
from behind on stowage shelves low beams
tight packing hull of ship no portholes
bucket of human waste out of reach
by head having rolled
in soiling dead air stench
darkness of filth
omens to spread
i cannot eat i pray to die
hot humid days nights joined
overboard plea away from moans
dysentery scurvy small pox doctor warns
let me kiss my darling girl one last time my special one
hold her tight against—away from vomit mucus blood
the man at my back who wont yet strangle me
like i wish like i beg
with no light for lives
dousing deaths transatlantic voyage
hammering silences of wrong
crimes—god never to be forgotten

From the Edge of Chaos and Form

2
my neck collared to plank flat on my back
palms at my thighs shoulder to shoulder on wood
hard shackled to women each side of me
one dead seems to be no chance rising
beyond another shelf
women stacked inches below overhead
suffocating twenty hour days here strap down screams
in outbursts waiting to crawl above board
flogging there before hose down naked
on quarterdeck crewmen to take me

tomorrow cask of poison

if not that
jump overboard
belong to no one

family im separated from never to see again
set my life free again on my own terms
follow without fear angels calling me
open   their wings I see as surest sign

hope   of my unfolding

3
i straddle wide a womans hips
between legs of a man behind
darkness everywhere cramped
we sit on wooden planks
naked bodies pressed
backs to chests
losing breath to heat
over a hundred degrees
ship sailing for americas
in cells three feet high
white men claim how lucky
and demand silence
or scourge us bad
to drag ours back to deck
for whip of bones through skin
too much now no more now
mama and papa gone
thrown port to starboard
frenzied the waters of reddening
here inside branded we are
one marked slave owner scar
burning here
to remember here
old woman up front
who cries at one behind
driving nails through scalp
she sings out
going down
down to jericho
on her way old woman
down soon to be free now
prayer found in nails cutting deep
deeper   into no more misery

The Doll

Blonde braids, embroidered headdress;
satin skirt, trim lace; red lips, drawn lashes—
my favorite doll I clutched to my chest

before letting go of Father's grip
from my dashing through the crowd
Auschwitz platform
for doll grabbed by SS soldier men—

rifles butting
my Father routed to throng of males
screaming all sides of me

"Gyere vissza! Marianna, a lányom!"
("Come back! Marianna, my daughter!")
arms outstretched beseeching
towards being dragged—shot—
bullet through temple
as twilight offering

my Father
my Father

only parent to my six-year-old body
gone, we were

with my young eyes—
Mengele mesmerized
ready to experiment—
different-colored irises
mine so unlike—

baby doll pieces thrown to pile
to be driven to children of Aryan blood

as old, humpbacked woman reassures me
that baby girl, my doll, will find a home
and be stitched and glued with love.
All will be well, she reminds
as she removes her bloody scarf

before one young nurse
next in stench of camp
I'm lured towards

disquietudes
that will save me
under skirt of her quiverings

to no injections, amputations,

already I'm a child of the disarticulated

From the Edge of Chaos and Form

Survivor

I know the darkness,
the meaning of the words my mother cannot tell
of where we're going, when I
—remember I was a girl
on no train to Germany but to Auschwitz.
Three-days' journey—cattle wagon floor
Hungarian transport through Slovakia.
Old, young, sick, somberness crammed in
terror of how no one talked.
My mother gripped my hand
and held tight to her chest my little sister
she tried to smile for. No station stops.
Buckets for water. Buckets for waste.
I ate no food my mother prepared.
Air slats high above—I focused on
light streaming in
as I prayed to go home, to hear
that everything would be all right,
to know that once those doors opened again
to blue sky that I wouldn't be ripped–
separated from my mother, sister–
soldiers forcing them away to gas chambers—
murder by asphyxiation before burning.
I should have held my mother's hand tighter,
so tight we became one
to meld into my sister's eyes of terror
that I might have softened in some final moment
always with her
and my mother, the endless years of wishing
I could have died with both of them.

The River

The river always wanders.
It trusts itself and finds a way.
It speaks another language of sound.
Its range is clear and murky.
This river has secrets it cannot tell.
Beneath the rippling surface,
rocks hold fast to sand
as I look for fish below.
The sun streams down
and I am weary,
wishing to be taken under,
to feel the grains of sand.
I want the coldness,
to be frozen,
to feel the waters through me
travel like a wave,
a ripple, a drop, a rush–
of knowing.

From the Edge of Chaos and Form

Acknowledgments

AllCreatures.org: "Taking Down the Bull," "Perception Ablation," "Stolen Property: Goosebumps from "Diamond Area," "The Shearing Floor," "Reptilian People," "Pangolin Endangerment," "Animal: Live Transport Airborne," "Battery Cage in Blackout House," "Artificial Insemination: Dairy Goat Method," "Elegy for the Horses," "In Honor of Sloths"

Backchannels Journal: "Definitions: Beautiful"

Consilience: "Chaos Theory"

Ekphrastic Review: "Disc to Disbeliefs"

Interalia Magazine: "Points of Ignition," "Sound, Intention, Moving Waters," "Identical Image Not Reflected upon Superimposition, "Earth Native," "Between a Star and a Planet," "Supermoon," "Lunar Eclipses," "Stolon: Plant Extension," "Tree Crown Decisiveness," "Waves of Iridescence"

Journal for Critical Animal Studies: "Animal: Living Soul"

Plants & Poetry: "Glowing Mushroom," "Honey Mushroom, Blue Mountains," "Sulphur Shelf on Western Hemlock"

Siamb! Issue #9: "Celestial Wakenings: Vincent van Gogh's *The Starry Night*"

Stick Figure Poetry Quarterly: "Boxes in Transit"

The Environmental Magazine: "Snowshoe Hare at Sunrise, Sunset," "*Da Ow Aga*: Edge of Lake Tahoe, Phrase of the Washoe Tribe," "Intimations of Bobcat," "School of Fish"

Tiny Seed Literary Journal: "Achene with Wings," "Dandelion," "Male Gentoo Penguin: Preparation for Incubation"

www.ingramcontent.com/pod-product-compliance
Lightning Source LLC
Chambersburg PA
CBHW071226090426
42736CB00014B/2992